# THE VALUE OF SOIL - 1

I0483086

MR VIVEK KUMAR PANDEY
SHAMBHUNATH

ISBN 978-1-63873-810-7

# Contents

# CHAPTER ONE

Tree

For other uses, see Tree (disambiguation).

Common ash (Fraxinus excelsior), a deciduous broad-leaved (angiosperm) tree

European larch (Larix decidua), a coniferous tree which is also deciduous

In botany, a tree is a perennial plant with an elongated stem, or trunk, supporting branches and leaves in most species. In some usages, the definition of a tree may be narrower, including only woody plants with secondary growth, plants that are usable as lumber or plants above a specified height. In wider definitions, the taller palms, tree ferns, bananas, and bamboos are also trees. Trees are not a taxonomic group but include a variety of plant species that have independently evolved a trunk and branches as a way to tower above other plants to compete for sunlight. Trees tend to be long-lived, some reaching several thousand years old. Trees have been in existence for 370 million years. It is estimated that there are just over 3 trillion mature trees in the world.[1]

A tree typically has many secondary branches supported clear of the ground by the trunk. This trunk typically contains woody tissue for strength, and vascular tissue to carry materials from one part of the tree to another. For most trees it is surrounded by a layer of bark which serves as a protective barrier. Below the ground, the roots branch and spread out widely; they serve to anchor the tree and extract moisture and nutrients from the soil. Above ground, the branches divide into smaller branches and shoots. The shoots typically bear leaves, which capture light energy and convert it into sugars by photosynthesis, providing the food for the tree's growth and development.

Trees usually reproduce using seeds. Flowers and fruit may be present, but some trees, such as conifers, instead have pollen cones and seed cones. Palms, bananas, and bamboos also produce seeds, but tree ferns produce spores instead.

Trees play a significant role in reducing erosion and moderating the climate. They remove carbon dioxide from the atmosphere and store large quantities of carbon in their tissues. Trees and forests provide a habitat for many species of animals and plants. Tropical rainforests are among the most biodiverse habitats in the world. Trees provide shade and shelter, timber for construction, fuel for cooking and heating, and fruit for food as well as having many other uses. In parts of the world, forests are shrinking as trees are cleared to increase the amount of land available for agriculture. Because of their longevity and usefulness, trees have always been revered, with sacred groves in various cultures, and they play a role in many of the world's mythologies.

Contents

Definition

Diagram of secondary growth in a eudicot or coniferous tree showing idealised vertical and horizontal sections. A new layer of wood is added in each growing season, thickening the stem, existing branches and roots.

Although "tree" is a term of common parlance, there is no universally recognised precise definition of what a tree is, either botanically or in common language.[2] In its broadest sense, a tree is any plant with the general form of an elongated stem, or trunk, which supports the photosynthetic leaves or branches at some distance above the ground.[3] Trees are also typically defined by height,[4] with smaller plants from 0.5 to 10 m (1.6 to 32.8 ft) being called shrubs,[5] so the minimum height of a tree is only loosely defined.[4] Large herbaceous plants such as papaya and bananas are trees in this broad sense.[2][6]

A commonly applied narrower definition is that a tree has a woody trunk formed by secondary growth, meaning that the trunk thickens each year by growing outwards, in addition to the primary upwards growth from the growing tip.[4][7] Under such a definition, herbaceous plants such as palms, bananas and papayas are not considered trees regardless of their height, growth form or stem girth. Certain monocots may be considered trees under a slightly looser definition;[8] while the Joshua tree, bamboos and palms do not have secondary growth and never produce true wood with growth rings,[9][10] they may produce "pseudo-wood" by lignifying cells formed by primary growth.[11] Tree species in the genus Dracaena, despite also being monocots, do have secondary growth caused by meristem in their trunk, but it is different from the thickening meristem found in dicotyledonous trees.[citation needed]

Aside from structural definitions, trees are commonly defined by use; for instance, as those plants which yield lumber.[12]

Overview

The tree growth habit is an evolutionary adaptation found in different groups of plants: by growing taller, trees are able to compete better for sunlight.[13] Trees tend to be tall and long-lived,[14] some reaching several thousand years old.[15] Several trees are among the oldest organisms now living.[16] Trees have modified structures such as thicker stems composed of specialised cells that add structural strength and durability, allowing them to grow taller than many other plants and to spread out their foliage. They differ from shrubs, which have a similar growth form, by usually growing larger and having a single main stem;[5] but there is no consistent distinction between a tree and a shrub,[17] made more confusing by the fact that trees may be reduced in size under harsher environmental conditions such as on mountains and subarctic areas. The tree form has evolved separately in unrelated classes of plants in response to similar environmental challenges, making it a classic example of parallel evolution. With an estimated 60,000-100,000 species, the number of trees worldwide might total twenty-five per cent of all living plant species.[18][19] The greatest number of these grow in tropical regions and many of these areas have not yet been fully surveyed by botanists, making tree diversity and ranges poorly known.[20]

Tall herbaceous monocotyledonous plants such as banana lack secondary growth, but are trees under the broadest definition.

The majority of tree species are angiosperms. There are about 1000 species of gymnosperm trees,[21] including conifers, cycads, ginkgophytes and gnetales; they produce seeds which are not enclosed in fruits, but in open structures such as pine cones, and many have tough waxy leaves, such as pine needles.[22] Most angiosperm trees are eudicots, the "true dicotyledons", so named because the seeds contain two cotyledons or seed leaves. There are also some trees among the old lineages of flowering plants called basal angiosperms or paleodicots; these include Amborella, Magnolia, nutmeg and avocado,[23] while trees such as bamboo, palms and bananas are monocots.

Wood gives structural strength to the trunk of most types of tree; this supports the plant as it grows larger. The vascular system of trees allows water, nutrients and other chemicals to be distributed around the plant, and without it trees would not be able to grow as large as they do. Trees, as relatively tall plants, need to draw water up the stem through the xylem from the roots by the suction produced as water evaporates from the leaves. If insufficient water is available the leaves will die.[24] The three main parts of trees include the root, stem, and leaves; they are integral parts of the vascular system which interconnects all the living cells. In trees and other plants that develop wood, the vascular cambium allows the expansion of vascular tissue that produces woody growth. Because this growth ruptures the epidermis of the stem, woody plants also have a cork cambium that develops among the phloem. The cork cambium gives rise to thickened cork cells to protect the surface of the plant and reduce water loss. Both the production of wood and the production of cork are forms of secondary growth.[25]

Trees are either evergreen, having foliage that persists and remains green throughout the year,[26] or deciduous, shedding their leaves at the end of the growing season and then having a dormant period without foliage.[27] Most conifers are evergreens, but larches (Larix and Pseudolarix) are deciduous, dropping their needles each autumn, and some species of cypress (Glyptostrobus, Metasequoia and Taxodium) shed small leafy shoots annually in a process known as cladoptosis.[5] The crown is the spreading top of a tree including the branches and leaves,[28] while the uppermost layer in a forest, formed by the crowns of the trees, is known as the canopy.[29] A sapling is a young tree.[30]

Many tall palms are herbaceous[31] monocots; these do not undergo secondary growth and never produce wood.[9][10] In many tall palms, the terminal bud on the main stem is the only one to develop, so they have unbranched trunks with large spirally arranged leaves. Some of the tree ferns, order Cyatheales, have tall straight trunks, growing up to 20 metres (66 ft), but these are composed not of wood but of rhizomes which grow vertically and are covered by numerous adventitious roots.[32]

Distribution

Further information: Forest

The Daintree Rainforest

The number of trees in the world, according to a 2015 estimate, is 3.04 trillion, of which 1.39 trillion (46%) are in the tropics or sub-tropics, 0.61 trillion (20%) in the temperate zones, and 0.74 trillion (24%) in the coniferous boreal forests. The estimate is about eight times higher than previous estimates, and is based on tree densities measured on over 400,000 plots. It remains subject to a wide margin of error, not least because the samples are mainly from Europe and North America. The estimate suggests that about 15 billion trees are cut down annually and about 5 billion are planted. In the 12,000 years since the start of human agriculture, the number of trees worldwide has decreased by 46%.[1][33][34][35]

In suitable environments, such as the Daintree Rainforest in Queensland, or the mixed podocarp and broadleaf forest of Ulva Island, New Zealand, forest is the more-or-less stable climatic climax community at the end of a plant succession, where open areas such as grassland are colonised by taller plants, which in turn give way to trees that eventually form a forest canopy.[36][37]

Conifers in the Swabian alps

In cool temperate regions, conifers often predominate; a widely distributed climax community in the far north of the northern hemisphere is moist taiga or northern coniferous forest (also called boreal forest).[38][39] Taiga is the world's largest land biome, forming 29% of the world's forest cover.[40] The long cold winter of the far north is unsuitable for plant growth and trees must grow rapidly in the short summer season when the temperature rises and the days are long. Light is very limited under their dense cover and there may be little plant life on the forest floor, although fungi may abound.[41] Similar woodland is found on mountains where the altitude causes the average temperature to be lower thus reducing the length of the growing season.[42]

Where rainfall is relatively evenly spread across the seasons in temperate regions, temperate broadleaf and mixed forest typified by species like oak, beech, birch and maple is found.[43] Temperate forest is also found in the southern hemisphere, as for example in the Eastern Australia temperate forest, characterised by Eucalyptus forest and open acacia woodland.[44]

In tropical regions with a monsoon or monsoon-like climate, where a drier part of the year alternates with a wet period as in the Amazon rainforest, different species of broad-leaved trees dominate the forest, some of them being deciduous.[45] In tropical regions with a drier savanna climate and insufficient rainfall to support dense forests, the canopy is not closed, and plenty of sunshine reaches the ground which is covered with grass and scrub. Acacia and baobab are well adapted to living in such areas.[46]

Parts and function

A young red pine (Pinus resinosa) with spread of roots visible, as a result of soil erosion

Roots

Main article: Root

The roots of a tree serve to anchor it to the ground and gather water and nutrients to transfer to all parts of the tree. They are also used for reproduction, defence, survival, energy storage and many other purposes. The radicle or embryonic root is the first part of a seedling to emerge from the seed during the process of germination. This develops into a taproot which goes straight downwards. Within a few weeks lateral roots branch out of the side of this and grow horizontally through the upper layers of the soil. In most trees, the taproot eventually withers away and the wide-spreading laterals remain. Near the tip of the finer roots are single cell root hairs. These are in immediate contact with the soil particles and can absorb water and nutrients such as potassium in solution. The roots require oxygen to respire and only a few species such as mangroves and the pond cypress (Taxodium ascendens) can live in permanently waterlogged soil.[47]

In the soil, the roots encounter the hyphae of fungi. Many of these are known as mycorrhiza and form a mutualistic relationship with the tree roots. Some are specific to a single tree species, which will not flourish in the absence of its mycorrhizal associate. Others are generalists and associate with many species. The tree acquires minerals such as phosphorus from the fungus, while the fungus obtains the carbohydrate products of photosynthesis from the tree.[48] The hyphae of the fungus can link different trees and a network is formed, transferring nutrients and signals from one place to another.[49] The fungus promotes growth of the roots and helps protect the trees against predators and pathogens. It can also limit damage done to a tree by pollution as the fungus accumulate heavy metals within its tissues.[50] Fossil evidence shows that roots have been associated with mycorrhizal fungi since the early Paleozoic, four hundred million years ago, when the first vascular plants colonised dry land.[51]

Buttress roots of the kapok tree (Ceiba pentandra)

Some trees such as the alders (Alnus species) have a symbiotic relationship with Frankia species, a filamentous bacterium that can fix nitrogen from the air, converting it into ammonia. They have actinorhizal root nodules on their roots in which the bacteria live. This process enables the tree to live in low nitrogen habitats where they would otherwise be unable to thrive.[52] The plant hormones called cytokinins initiate root nodule formation, in a process closely related to mycorrhizal association.[53]

It has been demonstrated that some trees are interconnected through their root system, forming a colony. The interconnections are made by the inosculation process, a kind of natural grafting or welding of vegetal tissues. The tests to demonstrate this networking are performed by injecting chemicals, sometimes radioactive, into a tree, and then checking for its presence in neighbouring trees.[54]

The roots are, generally, an underground part of the tree, but some tree species have evolved roots that are aerial. The common purposes for aerial roots may be of two kinds, to contribute to the mechanical stability of the tree, and to obtain oxygen from air. An instance of mechanical stability enhancement is the red mangrove that develops prop roots that loop out of the trunk and branches and descend vertically into the mud.[55] A similar structure is developed by the Indian banyan.[56] Many large trees have buttress roots which flare out from the lower part of the trunk. These brace the tree rather like angle brackets and provide stability, reducing sway in high winds. They are particularly prevalent in tropical rainforests where the soil is poor and the roots are close to the surface.[57]

Some tree species have developed root extensions that pop out of soil, in order to get oxygen, when it is not available in the soil because of excess water. These root extensions are called pneumatophores, and are present, among others, in black mangrove and pond cypress.[55]

Trunk

Northern beech (Fagus sylvatica) trunk in autumn

Main article: Trunk (botany)

The main purpose of the trunk is to raise the leaves above the ground, enabling the tree to overtop other plants and outcompete them for light.[58] It also transports water and nutrients from the roots to the aerial parts of the tree, and distributes the food produced by the leaves to all other parts, including the roots.[59]

In the case of angiosperms and gymnosperms, the outermost layer of the trunk is the bark, mostly composed of dead cells of phellem (cork).[60] It provides a thick, waterproof covering to the living inner tissue. It protects the trunk against the elements, disease, animal attack and fire. It is perforated by a large number of fine breathing pores called lenticels, through which oxygen diffuses. Bark is continually replaced by a living layer of cells called the cork cambium or phellogen.[60] The London plane (Platanus × acerifolia) periodically sheds its bark in large flakes. Similarly, the bark of the silver birch (Betula pendula) peels off in strips. As the tree's girth expands, newer layers of bark are larger in circumference, and the older layers develop fissures in many species. In some trees such as the pine (Pinus species) the bark exudes sticky resin which deters attackers whereas in rubber trees (Hevea brasiliensis) it is a milky latex that oozes out. The quinine bark tree (Cinchona officinalis) contains bitter substances to make the bark unpalatable.[59] Large tree-like plants with lignified trunks in the Pteridophyta, Arecales, Cycadophyta and Poales such as the tree ferns, palms, cycads and bamboos have different structures and outer coverings.[61]

A section of yew (Taxus baccata) showing 27 annual growth rings, pale sapwood and dark heartwood

Although the bark functions as a protective barrier, it is itself attacked by boring insects such as beetles. These lay their eggs in crevices and the larvae chew their way through the cellulose tissues leaving a gallery of tunnels. This may allow fungal spores to gain admittance and attack the tree. Dutch elm disease is caused by a fungus (Ophiostoma species) carried from one elm tree to another by various beetles. The tree reacts to the growth of the fungus by blocking off the xylem tissue carrying sap upwards and the branch above, and eventually the whole tree, is deprived of nourishment and dies. In Britain in the 1990s, 25 million elm trees were killed by this disease.[62]

The innermost layer of bark is known as the phloem and this is involved in the transport of the sap containing the sugars made by photosynthesis to other parts of the tree. It is a soft spongy layer of living cells, some of which are arranged end to end to form tubes. These are supported by parenchyma cells which provide padding and include fibres for strengthening the tissue.[63] Inside the phloem is a layer of undifferentiated cells one cell thick called the vascular cambium layer. The cells are continually dividing, creating phloem cells on the outside and wood cells known as xylem on the inside.[64]

The newly created xylem is the sapwood. It is composed of water-conducting cells and associated cells which are often living, and is usually pale in colour. It transports water and minerals from the roots to the upper parts of the tree. The oldest, inner part of the sapwood is progressively converted into heartwood as new sapwood is formed at the cambium. The conductive cells of the heartwood are blocked in some species. Heartwood is usually darker in colour than the sapwood. It is the dense central core of the trunk giving it rigidity. Three quarters of the dry mass of the xylem is cellulose, a polysaccharide, and most of the remainder is lignin, a complex polymer. A transverse section through a tree trunk or a horizontal core will show concentric circles or lighter or darker wood – tree rings.[65] These rings are the annual growth rings[66][67] There may also be rays running at right angles to growth rings. These are vascular rays which are thin sheets of living tissue permeating the wood.[65] Many older trees may become hollow but may still stand upright for many years.

Trees do not usually grow continuously throughout the year but mostly have spurts of active expansion followed by periods of rest. This pattern of growth is related to climatic conditions; growth normally ceases when conditions are either too cold or too dry. In readiness for the inactive period, trees form buds to protect the meristem, the zone of active growth. Before the period of dormancy, the last few leaves produced at the tip of a twig form scales. These are thick, small and closely wrapped and enclose the growing point in a waterproof sheath. Inside this bud there is a rudimentary stalk and neatly folded miniature leaves, ready to expand when the next growing season arrives. Buds also form in the axils of the leaves ready to produce new side shoots. A few trees, such as the eucalyptus, have "naked buds" with no protective scales and some conifers, such as the Lawson's cypress, have no buds but instead have little pockets of meristem concealed among the scale-like leaves.[69]

When growing conditions improve, such as the arrival of warmer weather and the longer days associated with spring in temperate regions, growth starts again. The expanding shoot pushes its way out, shedding the scales in the process. These leave behind scars on the surface of the twig. The whole year's growth may take place in just a few weeks. The new stem is unlignified at first and may be green and downy. The Arecaceae (palms) have their leaves spirally arranged on an unbranched trunk.[69] In some tree species in temperate climates, a second spurt of growth, a Lammas growth may occur which is believed to be a strategy to compensate for loss of early foliage to insect predators.[70]

Primary growth is the elongation of the stems and roots. Secondary growth consists of a progressive thickening and strengthening of the tissues as the outer layer of the epidermis is converted into bark and the cambium layer creates new phloem and xylem cells. The bark is inelastic.[71] Eventually the growth of a tree slows down and stops and it gets no taller. If damage occurs the tree may in time become hollow.[72]

Leaves

Main article: Leaf

Leaves are structures specialised for photosynthesis and are arranged on the tree in such a way as to maximise their exposure to light without shading each other.[73] They are an important investment by the tree and may be thorny or contain phytoliths, lignins, tannins or poisons to discourage herbivory. Trees have evolved leaves in a wide range of shapes and sizes, in response to environmental pressures including climate and predation. They can be broad or needle-like, simple or compound, lobed or entire, smooth or hairy, delicate or tough, deciduous or evergreen. The needles of coniferous trees are compact but are structurally similar to those of broad-leaved trees. They are adapted for life in environments where resources are low or water is scarce. Frozen ground may limit water availability and conifers are often found in colder places at higher altitudes and higher latitudes than broad leaved trees. In conifers such as fir trees, the branches hang down at an angle to the trunk, enabling them to shed snow. In contrast, broad leaved trees in temperate regions deal with winter weather by shedding their leaves. When the days get shorter and the temperature begins to decrease, the leaves no longer make new chlorophyll and the red and yellow pigments already present in the blades become apparent.[73] Synthesis in the leaf of a plant hormone called auxin also ceases. This causes the cells at the junction of the petiole and the twig to weaken until the joint breaks and the leaf floats to the ground. In tropical and subtropical regions, many trees keep their leaves all year round. Individual leaves may fall intermittently and be replaced by new growth but most leaves remain intact for some time. Other tropical species and those in arid regions may shed all their leaves annually, such as at the start of the dry season.[74] Many deciduous trees flower before the new leaves emerge.[75] A few trees do not have true leaves but instead have structures with similar external appearance such as Phylloclades – modified stem structures[76] – as seen in the genus

Phyllocladus.[77]

Reproduction

Further information: Plant reproduction, Pollination, and Seed dispersal

Trees can be pollinated either by wind or by animals, mostly insects. Many angiosperm trees are insect pollinated. Wind pollination may take advantage of increased wind speeds high above the ground.[78] Trees use a variety of methods of seed dispersal. Some rely on wind, with winged or plumed seeds. Others rely on animals, for example with edible fruits. Others again eject their seeds (ballistic dispersal), or use gravity so that seeds fall and sometimes roll.[79]

Seeds

Main article: Seed

Seeds are the primary way that trees reproduce and their seeds vary greatly in size and shape. Some of the largest seeds come from trees, but the largest tree, Sequoiadendron giganteum, produces one of the smallest tree seeds.[80] The great diversity in tree fruits and seeds reflects the many different ways that tree species have evolved to disperse their offspring.

Description:

https://upload.wikimedia.org/wikipedia/commons/thumb/6/60/Samara_olmo_frassino_acero.png/220px-Samara_olmo_frassino_acero.png

Wind dispersed seed of elm (Ulmus), ash (Fraxinus) and maple (Acer)

For a tree seedling to grow into an adult tree it needs light. If seeds only fell straight to the ground, competition among the concentrated saplings and the shade of the parent would likely prevent it from flourishing. Many seeds such as birch are small and have papery wings to aid dispersal by the wind. Ash trees and maples have larger seeds with blade shaped wings which spiral down to the ground when released. The kapok tree has cottony threads to catch the breeze.[81]

The seeds of conifers, the largest group of gymnosperms, are enclosed in a cone and most species have seeds that are light and papery that can be blown considerable distances once free from the cone.[82] Sometimes the seed remains in the cone for years waiting for a trigger event to liberate it. Fire stimulates release and germination of seeds of the jack pine, and also enriches the forest floor with wood ash and removes competing vegetation.[83] Similarly, a number of angiosperms including Acacia cyclops and Acacia mangium have seeds that germinate better after exposure to high temperatures.[84]

The flame tree Delonix regia does not rely on fire but shoots its seeds through the air when the two sides of its long pods crack apart explosively on drying.[81] The miniature cone-like catkins of alder trees produce seeds that contain small droplets of oil that help disperse the seeds on the surface of water. Mangroves often grow in water and some species have propagules, which are buoyant fruits with seeds that start germinating before becoming detached from the parent tree.[85][86] These float on the water and may become lodged on emerging mudbanks and successfully take root.[81]

Other seeds, such as apple pips and plum stones, have fleshy receptacles and smaller fruits like hawthorns have seeds enclosed in edible tissue; animals including mammals and birds eat the fruits and either discard the seeds, or swallow them so they pass through the gut to be deposited in the animal's droppings well away from the parent tree. The germination of some seeds is improved when they are processed in this way.[87] Nuts may be gathered by animals such as squirrels that cache any not immediately consumed.[88] Many of these caches are never revisited, the nut-casing softens with rain and frost, and the seed germinates in the spring.[89] Pine cones may similarly be hoarded by red squirrels, and grizzly bears may help to disperse the seed by raiding squirrel caches.[90]

The single extant species of Ginkgophyta (Ginkgo biloba) has fleshy seeds produced at the ends of short branches on female trees,[91] and Gnetum, a tropical and subtropical group of gymnosperms produce seeds at the tip of a shoot axis.[92]

Further information: Evolutionary history of plants

The earliest trees were tree ferns, horsetails and lycophytes, which grew in forests in the Carboniferous period. The first tree may have been Wattieza, fossils of which have been found in New York State in 2007 dating back to the Middle Devonian (about 385 million years ago). Prior to this discovery, Archaeopteris was the earliest known tree.[93] Both of these reproduced by spores rather than seeds and are considered to be links between ferns and the gymnosperms which evolved in the Triassic period. The gymnosperms include conifers, cycads, gnetales and ginkgos and these may have appeared as a result of a whole genome duplication event which took place about 319 million years ago.[94] Ginkgophyta was once a widespread diverse group[95] of which the only survivor is the maidenhair tree Ginkgo biloba. This is considered to be a living fossil because it is virtually unchanged from the fossilised specimens found in Triassic deposits.[96]

During the Mesozoic (245 to 66 million years ago) the conifers flourished and became adapted to live in all the major terrestrial habitats. Subsequently, the tree forms of flowering plants evolved during the Cretaceous period. These began to displace the conifers during the Tertiary era (66 to 2 million years ago) when forests covered the globe.[97] When the climate cooled 1.5 million years ago and the first of four ice ages occurred, the forests retreated as the ice advanced. In the interglacials, trees recolonised the land that had been covered by ice, only to be driven back again in the next ice age.[97]

Tree ecology

Further information: Forest

Trees are an important part of the terrestrial ecosystem,[98] providing essential habitats including many kinds of forest for communities of organisms. Epiphytic plants such as ferns, some mosses, liverworts, orchids and some species of parasitic plants (e.g., mistletoe) hang from branches;[99] these along with arboreal lichens, algae, and fungi provide micro-habitats for themselves and for other organisms, including animals. Leaves, flowers and fruits are seasonally available. On the ground underneath trees there is shade, and often there is undergrowth, leaf litter, and decaying wood that provide other habitat.[100][101] Trees stabilise the soil, prevent rapid run-off of rain water, help prevent desertification, have a role in climate control and help in the maintenance of biodiversity and ecosystem balance.[102]

Many species of tree support their own specialised invertebrates. In their natural habitats, 284 different species of insect have been found on the English oak (Quercus robur)[103] and 306 species of invertebrate on the Tasmanian oak (Eucalyptus obliqua).[104] Non-native tree species provide a less biodiverse community, for example in the United Kingdom the sycamore (Acer pseudoplatanus), which originates from southern Europe, has few associated invertebrate species, though its bark supports a wide range of lichens, bryophytes and other epiphytes.[105]

In ecosystems such as mangrove swamps, trees play a role in developing the habitat, since the roots of the mangrove trees reduce the speed of flow of tidal currents and trap water-borne sediment, reducing the water depth and creating suitable conditions for further mangrove colonisation. Thus mangrove swamps tend to extend seawards in suitable locations.[106] Mangrove swamps also provide an effective buffer against the more damaging effects of cyclones and tsunamis.[107]

Uses

Silviculture is the practice of controlling the establishment, growth, composition, health, and quality of forests, which are areas that have a high density of trees. Cultivated trees are planted and tended by humans, usually because they provide food (fruits or nuts), ornamental beauty, or some type of wood product that benefits people. An area of land planted with fruit or nut trees is an orchard.[108] A small wooded area, usually with no undergrowth, is called a grove[109] and a small wood or thicket of trees and bushes is called a coppice or copse.[110] A large area of land covered with trees and undergrowth is called woodland or forest.[111] An area of woodland composed primarily of trees established by planting or artificial seeding is known as a plantation.[112]

Food

Further information: nut (fruit) and fruit

Trees are the source of many of the world's best known fleshy fruits. Apples, pears, plums, cherries and citrus are all grown commercially in temperate climates and a wide range of edible fruits are found in the tropics. Other commercially important fruit include dates, figs and olives. Palm oil is obtained from the fruits of the oil palm (Elaeis guineensis). The fruits of the cocoa tree (Theobroma cacao) are used to make cocoa and chocolate and the berries of coffee trees, Coffea arabica and Coffea canephora, are processed to extract the coffee beans. In many rural areas of the world, fruit is gathered from forest trees for consumption.[113] Many trees bear edible nuts which can loosely be described as being large, oily kernels found inside a hard shell. These include coconuts (Cocos nucifera), Brazil nuts (Bertholletia excelsa), pecans (Carya illinoinensis), hazel nuts (Corylus), almonds (Prunus dulcis), walnuts (Juglans regia), pistachios (Pistacia vera) and many others. They are high in nutritive value and contain high-quality protein, vitamins and minerals as well as dietary fibre.[114] A variety of nut oils are extracted by pressing for culinary use; some such as walnut, pistachio and hazelnut oils are prized for their distinctive flavours, but they tend to spoil quickly.[115]

Description:
https://upload.wikimedia.org/
wikipedia/commons/thumb/9/9a/
Maple_syrup_taps.jpg/220px-
Maple_syrup_taps.jpg

Sugar maple (Acer saccharum) tapped to collect sap for maple syrup

In temperate climates there is a sudden movement of sap at the end of the winter as trees prepare to burst into growth. In North America, the sap of the sugar maple (Acer saccharum) is most often used in the production of a sweet liquid, maple syrup. About 90% of the sap is water, the remaining 10% being a mixture of various sugars and certain minerals. The sap is harvested by drilling holes in the trunks of the trees and collecting the liquid that flows out of the inserted spigots. It is piped to a sugarhouse where it is heated to concentrate it and improve its flavour. Similarly in northern Europe the spring rise in the sap of the silver birch (Betula pendula) is tapped and collected, either to be drunk fresh or fermented into an alcoholic drink. In Alaska, the sap of the sweet birch (Betula lenta) is made into a syrup with a sugar content of 67%. Sweet birch sap is more dilute than maple sap; a hundred litres are required to make one litre of birch syrup.[116]

Various parts of trees are used as spices. These include cinnamon, made from the bark of the cinnamon tree (Cinnamomum zeylanicum) and allspice, the dried small fruits of the pimento tree (Pimenta dioica). Nutmeg is a seed found in the fleshy fruit of the nutmeg tree (Myristica fragrans) and cloves are the unopened flower buds of the clove tree (Syzygium aromaticum).[117]

Many trees have flowers rich in nectar which are attractive to bees. The production of forest honey is an important industry in rural areas of the developing world where it is undertaken by small-scale beekeepers using traditional methods.[118] The flowers of the elder (Sambucus) are used to make elderflower cordial and petals of the plum (Prunus spp.) can be candied.[119] Sassafras oil is a flavouring obtained from distilling bark from the roots of the sassafras tree (Sassafras albidum).

The leaves of trees are widely gathered as fodder for livestock and some can be eaten by humans but they tend to be high in tannins which makes them bitter. Leaves of the curry tree (Murraya koenigii) are eaten, those of kaffir lime (Citrus × hystrix) (in Thai food)[120] and Ailanthus (in Korean dishes such as bugak) and those of the European bay tree (Laurus nobilis) and the California bay tree (Umbellularia californica) are used for flavouring food.[117] Camellia sinensis, the source of tea, is a small tree but seldom reaches its full height, being heavily pruned to make picking the leaves easier.[121]

Wood smoke can be used to preserve food. In the hot smoking process the food is exposed to smoke and heat in a controlled environment. The food is ready to eat when the process is complete, having been tenderised and flavoured by the smoke it has absorbed. In the cold process, the temperature is not allowed to rise above 100 °F (38 °C). The flavour of the food is enhanced but raw food requires further cooking. If it is to be preserved, meat should be cured before cold smoking.[122]

Fuel

Main article: Wood fuel

Description:
https://upload.wikimedia.org/
wikipedia/commons/thumb/1/12/
Selling_fuelwood.jpeg/220px-
Selling_fuelwood.jpeg

Selling firewood at a market

Wood has traditionally been used for fuel, especially in rural areas. In less developed nations it may be the only fuel available and collecting firewood is often a time consuming task as it becomes necessary to travel further and further afield in the search for fuel.[123] It is often burned inefficiently on an open fire. In more developed countries other fuels are available and burning wood is a choice rather than a necessity. Modern wood-burning stoves are very fuel efficient and new products such as wood pellets are available to burn.[124]

Charcoal can be made by slow pyrolysis of wood by heating it in the absence of air in a kiln. The carefully stacked branches, often oak, are burned with a very limited amount of air. The process of converting them into charcoal takes about fifteen hours. Charcoal is used as a fuel in barbecues and by blacksmiths and has many industrial and other uses.[125]

Timber

Timber, "trees that are grown in order to produce wood"[126] is cut into lumber (sawn wood) for use in construction. Wood has been an important, easily available material for construction since humans started building shelters. Engineered wood products are available which bind the particles, fibres or veneers of wood together with adhesives to form composite materials. Plastics have taken over from wood for some traditional uses.[127]

Wood is used in the construction of buildings, bridges, trackways, piles, poles for power lines, masts for boats, pit props, railway sleepers, fencing, hurdles, shuttering for concrete, pipes, scaffolding and pallets. In housebuilding it is used in joinery, for making joists, roof trusses, roofing shingles, thatching, staircases, doors, window frames, floor boards, parquet flooring, panelling and cladding.

Wood is used to construct carts, farm implements, boats, dugout canoes and in shipbuilding. It is used for making furniture, tool handles, boxes, ladders, musical instruments, bows, weapons, matches, clothes pegs, brooms, shoes, baskets, turnery, carving, toys, pencils, rollers, cogs, wooden screws, barrels, coffins, skittles, veneers, artificial limbs, oars, skis, wooden spoons, sports equipment and wooden balls.[128]

Wood is pulped for paper and used in the manufacture of cardboard and made into engineered wood products for use in construction such as fibreboard, hardboard, chipboard and plywood.[128] The wood of conifers is known as softwood while that of broad-leaved trees is hardwood.[129]

Besides inspiring artists down the centuries, trees have been used to create art. Living trees have been used in bonsai and in tree shaping, and both living and dead specimens have been sculpted into sometimes fantastic shapes.[130]

Bonsai

Main article: Bonsai

Bonsai (盆栽, lit. The art of growing a miniature tree or trees in a low-sided pot or tray) is the practice of hòn non bộ originated in China and spread to Japan more than a thousand years ago, there are similar practices in other cultures like the living miniature landscapes of Vietnam hòn non bộ. The word bonsai is often used in English as an umbrella term for all miniature trees in containers or pots.[131]

The purposes of bonsai are primarily contemplation (for the viewer) and the pleasant exercise of effort and ingenuity (for the grower).[132] Bonsai practice focuses on long-term cultivation and shaping of one or more small trees growing in a container, beginning with a cutting, seedling, or small tree of a species suitable for bonsai development. Bonsai can be created from nearly any perennial woody-stemmed tree or shrub species[133] that produces true branches and can be cultivated to remain small through pot confinement with crown and root pruning. Some species are popular as bonsai material because they have characteristics, such as small leaves or needles, that make them appropriate for the compact visual scope of bonsai and a miniature deciduous forest can even be created using such species as Japanese maple, Japanese zelkova or hornbeam.[134]

Tree shaping

Tree shaping is the practice of changing living trees and other woody plants into man made shapes for art and useful structures. There are a few different methods[135] of shaping a tree. There is a gradual method and there is an instant method. The gradual method slowly guides the growing tip along predetermined pathways over time whereas the instant method bends and weaves saplings 2 to 3 m (6.6 to 9.8 ft) long into a shape that becomes more rigid as they thicken up.[136] Most artists use grafting of living trunks, branches, and roots, for art or functional structures and there are plans to grow "living houses" with the branches of trees knitting together to give a solid, weatherproof exterior combined with an interior application of straw and clay to provide a stucco-like inner surface.[136]

Tree shaping has been practised for at least several hundred years, the oldest known examples being the living root bridges built and maintained by the Khasi people of Meghalaya, India using the roots of the rubber tree (Ficus elastica).[137][138]

Cork is produced from the thick bark of the cork oak (Quercus suber). It is harvested from the living trees about once every ten years in an environmentally sustainable industry.[139] More than half the world's cork comes from Portugal and is largely used to make stoppers for wine bottles.[140] Other uses include floor tiles, bulletin boards, balls, footwear, cigarette tips, packaging, insulation and joints in woodwind instruments.[140]

The bark of other varieties of oak has traditionally been used in Europe for the tanning of hides though bark from other species of tree has been used elsewhere. The active ingredient, tannin, is extracted and after various preliminary treatments, the skins are immersed in a series of vats containing solutions in increasing concentrations. The tannin causes the hide to become supple, less affected by water and more resistant to bacterial attack.[141]

At least 120 drugs come from plant sources, many of them from the bark of trees.[142] Quinine originates from the cinchona tree (Cinchona) and was for a long time the remedy of choice for the treatment of malaria.[143] Aspirin was synthesised to replace the sodium salicylate derived from the bark of willow trees (Salix) which had unpleasant side effects.[144] The anti-cancer drug Paclitaxel is derived from taxol, a substance found in the bark of the Pacific yew (Taxus brevifolia).[145] Other tree based drugs come from the paw-paw (Carica papaya), the cassia (Cassia spp.), the cocoa tree (Theobroma cacao), the tree of life (Camptotheca acuminata) and the downy birch (Betula pubescens).[142]

The papery bark of the white birch tree (Betula papyrifera) was used extensively by Native Americans. Wigwams were covered by it and canoes were constructed from it. Other uses included food containers, hunting and fishing equipment, musical instruments, toys and sledges.[146] Nowadays, bark chips, a by-product of the timber industry, are used as a mulch and as a growing medium for epiphytic plants that need a soil-free compost.

Ornamental trees

Main article: Ornamental trees

Trees create a visual impact in the same way as do other landscape features and give a sense of maturity and permanence to park and garden. They are grown for the beauty of their forms, their foliage, flowers, fruit and bark and their siting is of major importance in creating a landscape. They can be grouped informally, often surrounded by plantings of bulbs, laid out in stately avenues or used as specimen trees. As living things, their appearance changes with the season and from year to year.[148]

Trees are often planted in town environments where they are known as street trees or amenity trees. They can provide shade and cooling through evapotranspiration, absorb greenhouse gases and pollutants, intercept rainfall, and reduce the risk of flooding. It has been shown that they are beneficial to humans in creating a sense of well-being and reducing stress. Many towns have initiated tree-planting programmes.[149] In London for example, there is an initiative to plant 20,000 new street trees and to have an increase in tree cover of 5% by 2025, equivalent to one tree for every resident.[150]

latex collecting from a rubber tree (Hevea brasiliensis)

Further information: Resin, Latex, and Camphor

Latex is a sticky defensive secretion that protects plants against herbivores. Many trees produce it when injured but the main source of the latex used to make natural rubber is the Pará rubber tree (Hevea brasiliensis). Originally used to create bouncy balls and for the waterproofing of cloth, natural rubber is now mainly used in tyres for which synthetic materials have proved less durable.[151] The latex exuded by the balatá tree (Manilkara bidentata) is used to make golf balls and is similar to gutta-percha, made from the latex of the "getah perca" tree Palaquium. This is also used as an insulator, particularly of undersea cables, and in dentistry, walking sticks and gun butts. It has now largely been replaced by synthetic materials.[152]

Resin is another plant exudate that may have a defensive purpose. It is a viscous liquid composed mainly of volatile terpenes and is produced mostly by coniferous trees. It is used in varnishes, for making small castings and in ten-pin bowling balls. When heated, the terpenes are driven off and the remaining product is called "rosin" and is used by stringed instrumentalists on their bows. Some resins contain essential oils and are used in incense and aromatherapy. Fossilised resin is known as amber and was mostly formed in the Cretaceous (145 to 66 million years ago) or more recently. The resin that oozed out of trees sometimes trapped insects or spiders and these are still visible in the interior of the amber.[153]

The camphor tree (Cinnamomum camphora) produces an essential oil[117] and the eucalyptus tree (Eucalyptus globulus) is the main source of eucalyptus oil which is used in medicine, as a fragrance and in industry.[154]

Care

Dead trees pose a safety risk, especially during high winds and severe storms, and removing dead trees involves a financial burden, whereas the presence of healthy trees can clean the air, increase property values, and reduce the temperature of the built environment and thereby reduce building cooling costs. During times of drought, trees can fall into water stress, which may cause a tree to become more susceptible to disease and insect problems, and ultimately may lead to a tree's death. Irrigating trees during dry periods can reduce the risk of water stress and death.[155]

Mythology

ggdrasil, the World Ash of Norse mythology

Trees have been venerated since time immemorial. To the ancient Celts, certain trees, especially the oak, ash and thorn, held special significance[156] as providing fuel, building materials, ornamental objects and weaponry. Other cultures have similarly revered trees, often linking the lives and fortunes of individuals to them or using them as oracles. In Greek mythology, dryads were believed to be shy nymphs who inhabited trees.

The Oubangui people of west Africa plant a tree when a child is born. As the tree flourishes, so does the child but if the tree fails to thrive, the health of the child is considered at risk. When it flowers it is time for marriage. Gifts are left at the tree periodically and when the individual dies, their spirit is believed to live on in the tree.[157]

Trees have their roots in the ground and their trunk and branches extended towards the sky. This concept is found in many of the world's religions as a tree which links the underworld and the earth and holds up the heavens. In Norse mythology, Yggdrasil is a central cosmic tree whose roots and branches extend to various worlds. Various creatures live on it.[158] In India, Kalpavriksha is a wish-fulfilling tree, one of the nine jewels that emerged from the primitive ocean. Icons are placed beneath it to be worshipped, tree nymphs inhabit the branches and it grants favours to the devout who tie threads round the trunk.[159] Democracy started in North America when the Great Peacemaker formed the Iroquois Confederacy, inspiring the warriors of the original five American nations to bury their weapons under the Tree of Peace, an eastern white pine (Pinus strobus).[160] In the creation story in the Bible, the tree of life and the knowledge of good and evil was planted by God in the Garden of Eden.[161]

Sacred groves exist in China, India, Africa and elsewhere. They are places where the deities live and where all the living things are either sacred or are companions of the gods. Folklore lays down the supernatural penalties that will result if desecration takes place for example by the felling of trees. Because of their protected status, sacred groves may be the only relics of ancient forest and have a biodiversity much greater than the surrounding area.[162] Some Ancient Indian tree deities, such as Puliyidaivalaiyamman, the Tamil deity of the tamarind tree, or Kadambariyamman, associated with the kadamba tree were seen as manifestations of a goddess who offers her blessings by giving fruits in abundance.[163]

The General Sherman Tree, thought to be the world's largest by volume

Main article: List of superlative trees

Trees have a theoretical maximum height of 130 m (430 ft),[164] but the tallest known specimen on earth is believed to be a coast redwood (Sequoia sempervirens) at Redwood National Park, California. It has been named Hyperion and is 115.85 m (380.1 ft) tall.[165] In 2006, it was reported to be 379.1 ft (115.5 m) tall.[166] The tallest known broad-leaved tree is a mountain ash (Eucalyptus regnans) growing in Tasmania with a height of 99.8 m (327 ft).[167]

The largest tree by volume is believed to be a giant sequoia (Sequoiadendron giganteum) known as the General Sherman Tree in the Sequoia National Park in Tulare County, California. Only the trunk is used in the calculation and the volume is estimated to be 1,487 m3 (52,500 cu ft).[168]

The oldest living tree with a verified age is also in California. It is a Great Basin bristlecone pine (Pinus longaeva) growing in the White Mountains. It has been dated by drilling a core sample and counting the annual rings. It is estimated to currently be 5,069 years old.[a][169]

A little farther south, at Santa Maria del Tule, Oaxaca, Mexico, is the tree with the broadest trunk. It is a Montezuma cypress (Taxodium mucronatum) known as Árbol del Tule and its diameter at breast height is 11.62 m (38.1 ft) giving it a girth of 36.2 m (119 ft). The tree's trunk is far from round and the exact dimensions may be misleading as the circumference includes much empty space between